Gadirok

REQUIEM CHORUS

HWANG JEONG-HO

Gadirok
REQUIEM CHORUS 1
HWANG JEONG-HO

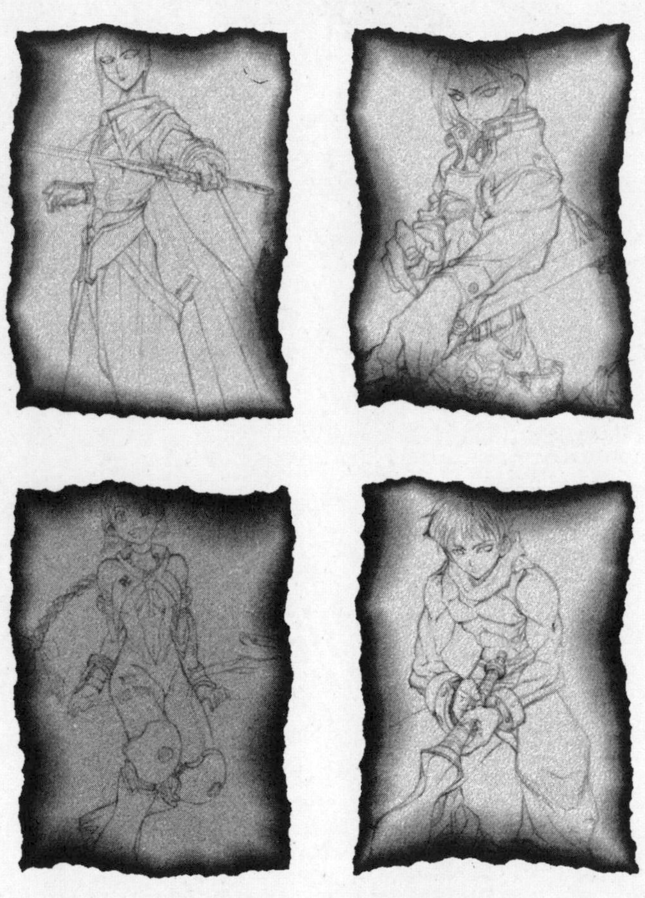

YOU LIKE THE RAIN?
YOU KNOW WHY?
I DON'T LIKE IT.
IT REMINDS ME OF WHINING PEASANTS, WHO STINK OF THE SEWER AND BEG FOR MONEY.

GAT! SCHEMING TO MOVE UP THE RANKS BY BECOMING THE PRINCE'S PET... YOU'RE NOTHING BUT A **PEASANT**!

HE...HE'S HERE!
GAT!

REINFORCEMENTS JUST LEFT HEADQUARTERS!
HE KILLED ALL THOSE SOLDIERS SINGLE-HANDEDLY...
NO,
IT'S TOO LATE.
PEASANTS SHOULD LIVE AND DIE LIKE PEASANTS!
FWOOOSH

THWOMP

GASP! JUST LIKE I EXPECTED!

THWOMP

BLRR-GH!

I FORGOT...

Y-YOU'RE LEFT-HANDED.

GAT,
A PEASANT WHO REFUSED TO LIVE LIKE ONE.
THE IDIOT KING, BEFRIENDING TRASH LIKE YOU AND PLACING THEM IN THE CENTER OF POWER...
FOOL! THAT'S WHAT THREW THE JEW-SHIN FAMILY INTO TURMOIL! BUT IT WAS THE HEROIC ACTS OF GENERAL HAE-MO-SOO THAT ASSURED ITS DOWNFALL.
EVEN PRINCE CHI-WOO, YOUR LAST HOPE, HAS BECOME DERANGED...
SKLRSSH

SKLRSCH

ARGH!

THWUMP

HEY GAT, WE'RE FRIENDS, RIGHT? DON'T FORGET WHO USED TO TAKE FOOD TO YOUR FAMILY...

철 컹
CREAKKKK
GROWRR
캬아
Y-YOUR HIGHNESS!

IT HURTS ...
ARGHHH!

THIS IS THE FIRST TIME I'VE EVER SEEN ROYALTY THIS CLOSE!
HOW AMAZING! HE'S GOT ARMS AND LEGS JUST LIKE US!
I THOUGHT THEY HAD WINGS...

SO THIS IS THE FUTURE EMPEROR? WOW!
FHWP
FHWP

HMM... ARE YOU REALLY A PRINCE? YOU CERTAINLY DON'T LOOK LIKE ONE.
SO-AH!
WHA?!
GRANDPA!!
DID YOU FINISH ALL THE CHORES I'VE ASSIGNED YOU?
O-OF COURSE.
FWSSSSH
AHEH...I THINK I'LL GO CHECK IF THINGS ARE STILL IN ORDER.

Are you ready?!
How dare you address him so rudely?!
I'm with you.
내가 함께 해주지.
It's okay. **She** was rude at first, also.
죽는다는 거
사는 것만큼 힘든 일이야.
지금은 참고 버텨내야 해...
Dying is just as difficult as staying alive. For now, we must endure the hardships...

GRAB!

I-IF YOU WERE GOING TO END UP LIKE THIS, THEN WHY DID YOU EVEN BOTHER TELLING ME ALL THOSE THINGS?!

WHY THE HELL DID YOU SAY THOSE THINGS, WHEN YOU WERE JUST GOING TO **COLLAPSE** ON ME?!

AAAH!
THWAP
THWAP
?!
WAAAAH!!

AAH!

NOW IS NOT THE TIME. LET US NOT ACT HASTILY.

YES, YES... PLEASE DON'T WORRY, YOUR HIGHNESS. NO ONE HERE WILL DARE HARM YOU.

YOU KNOW THAT BETTER THAN ANYONE ELSE. SO PLEASE, HAVE PATIENCE.

HIS SUFFERING MUST BE IMMENSE, FOR HE HAS WITNESSED THE DEATHS OF HIS LOVED ONES AS THE RESULT OF THE CONSPIRACY OF HAE-MO-SOO.
HOWEVER, HE WILL NOT REMAIN IN THIS STATE FOREVER, SINCE HIS HIGHNESS IS A PERSON OF GREAT STRENGTH.

KER-BLAM
shKRACK
I JUST DON'T UNDER-STAND GRANDPA.
WHY DOES HE MAKE ME PRACTICE MARTIAL ARTS AND DO CHORES LIKE THIS?!
A GIRL SHOULDN'T HAVE TO DO THESE THINGS!
shPAK

AH--! I WISH I COULD HAVE THE LIFE OF A NORMAL GIRL!

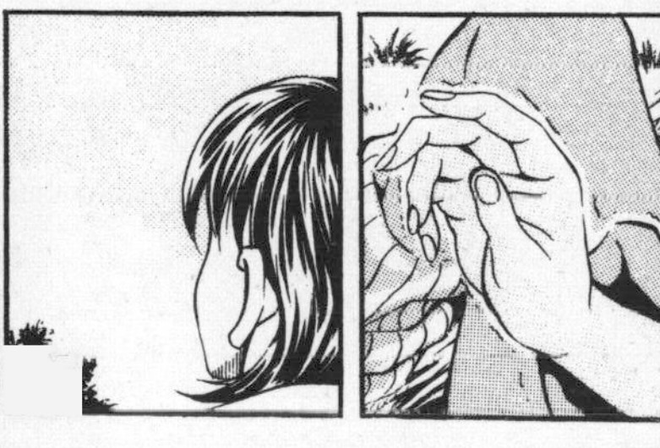

IT WAS ACTUALLY SCARY.

I'VE NEVER MET ANYONE WHO HAD SO MUCH ENERGY SWIRLING INSIDE THEIR BODY. IT FELT AS IF MY ENERGY WOULD BE **ENGULFED** BY IT...

PERHAPS **THAT'S** ROYAL HERITAGE.

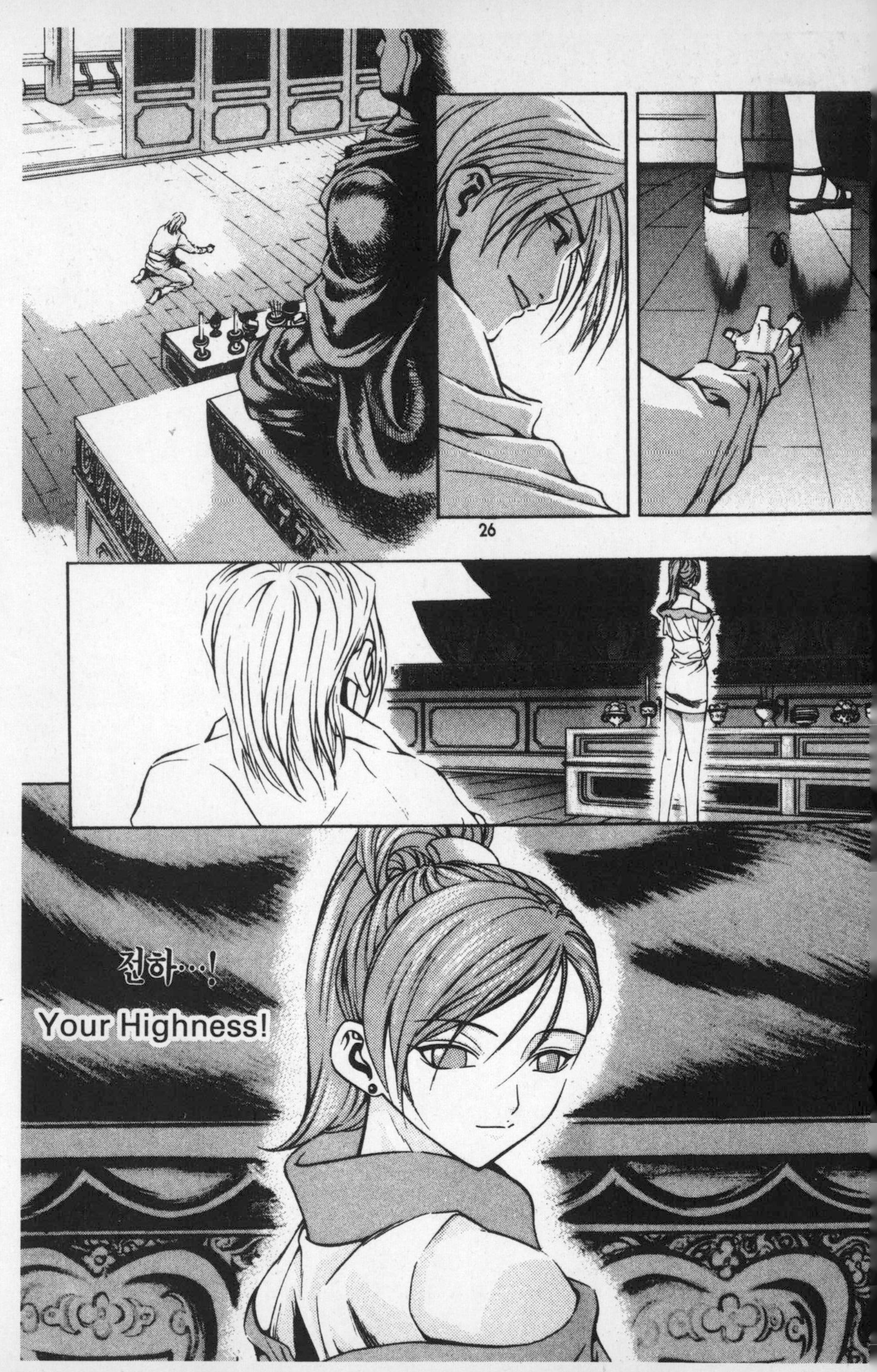
26
전하…!
Your Highness!

서 뭐 하는 거야?
서니가 말이
잖아.
Hey, what're you doing here? You look like hell.
한심하군. 기껏 살려놨더니 고작 한다는 게 벌레잡기냐.
Pathetic. We didn't save you so you can catch **bugs**!
AAH...
Wipe that stupid smile off your face! It was you.

우릴 죽인 건…!
It was YOU who killed us!!

우워어!
GRAAARGH!
여기서 꺼내 줘,
추워! 어두워!
죽기 싫어!
LET US OUT!
IT'S SO COLD AND DARK!
WE DON'T WANT TO DIE!
I-I'm so sorry, everyone.
I'm so sorry…

AAAH! NOW **THAT'S** WATER!
I'VE TRAVELED TO MANY PLACES, BUT I NEVER THOUGHT THERE'D BE SUCH GREAT TASTING WATER SO CLOSE!

?!

BAHRON!

YOU CONNIVING TRAITOR!

TRAITOR?

HMPH! THERE'S NO SUCH THING AS **TREASON** TO AN ASSASSIN.
AN ASSASSIN SIDES WITH ANYONE WHO HAS MONEY AND POWER.

ANYHOW, SORRY, BUT LORD HAE-MO-SOO WANTS EVERYONE INVOLVED WITH THE PRINCE **ELIMINATED**.

아아아아
BWOOOOMPF

AAAARGH!!!
AAAH!

KRACK

THWUMP
THAT WAS CLOSE! SORRY I'M LATE, YOUR HIGHNESS. I HAD TO TAKE CARE OF SOME THINGS.
WHY, YOU LITTLE...!
STUPID LITTLE GIRL! MAYBE I'LL HAVE SOME FUN WITH YOU BEFORE I KILL YOU!
HEY! GET YOUR MIND OUT OF THE GUTTER, PERVERT!
阿彌陀佛！釋迦如來佛！普提尊佛！鐵甲將軍！
鐵板道人！鳥衣仙人！
鐵甲將軍！日月神！五雷神將！
WOW! A SPELL!

36

WHAT BRINGS YOU SOLDIERS TO OUR SACRED TEMPLE?
GREETINGS, GREAT GENERAL TAI-GONG-WANG.
DO YOU KNOW WHO I AM?

AT LEAST DROP YOUR SWORD AND RUN, OR IS THAT TOO HUMILIATING FOR YOU, GAT?
SHUT UP!
YOU BELIEVE LIFE HAS ONLY ONE PATH! THAT'S WHY YOU WON'T SURVIVE IN THIS WORLD!
SHWSSH
콱
SHKRAK
!
I KNEW I SHOULDN'T HAVE TRUSTED YOU...
Trust is an excuse for the weak. Only FOOLISH people rely on trust.
YOU MUST BE HUMILIA-TED, ALSO.

THAT'S WHY YOU'RE MAKING THOSE POOR EXCUSES TO JUSTIFY YOURSELF!
AARGH!
SHWACK

I AM OF THE SOO-RA FAMILY.
YOU SEEM A LITTLE TOO YOUNG TO KNOW WHO I AM.
AAH, THE ONES BLESSED WITH LONGEVITY.
THE SOO-RA FAMILY... THAT'S A NAME DEAR TO MY HEART, A NAME I ONCE SHARED A MEANINGFUL CONNECTION WITH.
GENERAL! THE ERA OF THE HWAN-WOONG DYNASTY IS OVER. I'VE ALSO HEARD THE PRINCE IS NOT LIKELY TO RECOVER.
THUS, I ASK FOR YOUR COOPERATION.
I'M AFRAID I CANNOT. THOUGH HE IS NOT WELL, HAVING ONCE BEEN A ROYAL GUARD OF THE DYNASTY, IT IS MY DUTY TO PROTECT HIS HIGHNESS.
EVEN IF I HAVE TO SACRIFICE MY LIFE.
WELL, THEN...

PLEASE PARDON MY INSOLENCE!
AARGH! AM I STILL ALIVE?!
FHWP
HUH?
DIVINE PROTECTION TALISMAN?! THIS BELONGS TO THE MASTER... HOW DID THIS GET IN HERE?
THEN THE MASTER...?!
WAIT!

GWORRRR
I ORDER ALL OF YOU TO LEAVE!

SHWOOOSH

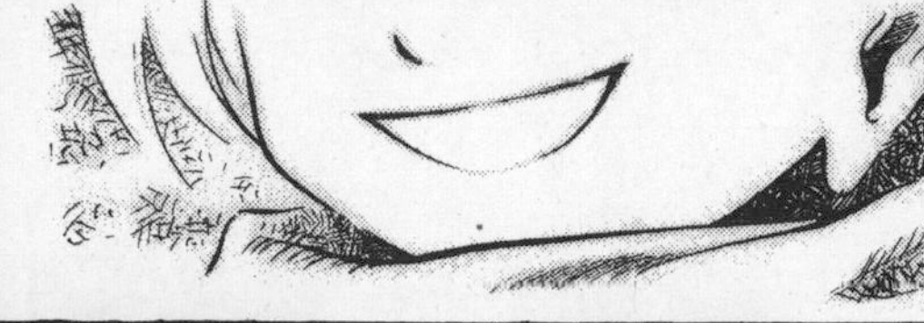
I wanna be just like
General Tai-Gong-Wang
when I grow up!

GENERAL!!!

Mother,
why must I call
him general?
Do not harbor any
hatred or hold any
grudge against him, my
dear. He's a Royal
Guard of the Emperor,
a responsibility we
must not prevent him
from fulfilling.

YOU AND THAT STUPID PRINCE...
CAN GO TO HELL!
!
RATHER A FRAIL CHILD!

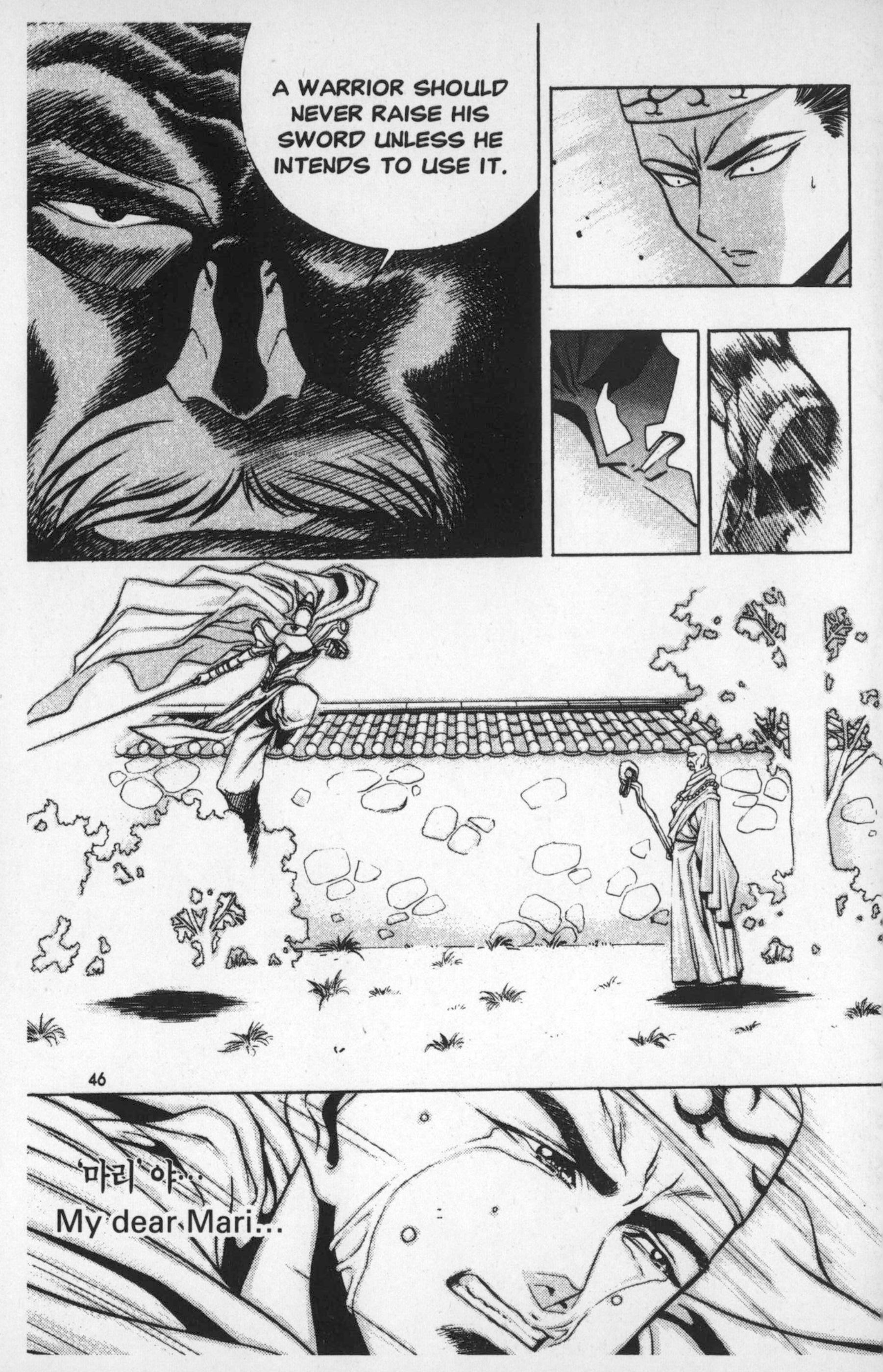
A WARRIOR SHOULD NEVER RAISE HIS SWORD UNLESS HE INTENDS TO USE IT.
'마리' 야...
My dear Mari...

너의 아버지는…
Your father is
이 나라 제일의
장군이시란다.
the greatest general
of this dynasty.
ker-KRACK
Father…
W…Why did you abandon mother?

A FACE I'VE BEEN YEARNING FOR...

GENERAL MARI!
HOW DID THAT OLD MAN...?!

HAHA, ALL OF YOU ARE PLANNING TO FIGHT THIS OLD MAN? WHAT AM I TO DO, FOR IT'S EASIER FOR ME TO **KILL** YOU THAN LET YOU LIVE.
FLINCH
주춤

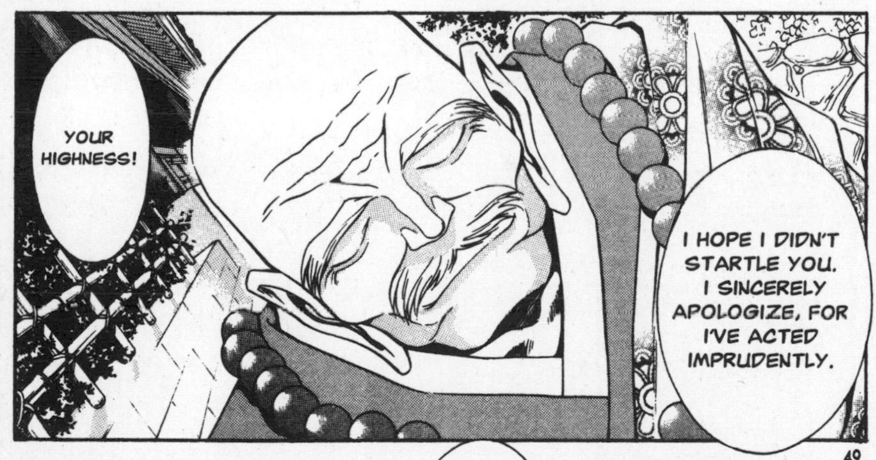
I HOPE I DIDN'T STARTLE YOU. I SINCERELY APOLOGIZE, FOR I'VE ACTED IMPRUDENTLY.
YOUR HIGHNESS!

ALLOW ME TO ESCORT YOUR HIGHNESS TO A SAFE PLACE.

SO, PLEASE...
G-GRANDPA!
TSK, TSK. MARI MUST'VE UNDERESTIMATED THIS OLD MAN.

HOWEVER, IT'S RATHER **SURPRISING** TO SEE THE ONCE GREAT GENERAL OF THIS DYNASTY TO BE INCAPABLE OF SENSING SOMEONE APPROACHING FROM BEHIND...
I GUESS YOU'VE GOTTEN OLD.
GRAB
GO!
YOU MUST PROTECT HIS HIGHNESS AT **ALL** COST! WE CANNOT AFFORD TO LOSE THE ONLY HOPE FOR THIS LAND.
BUT...

GRANDPA!
I CAN'T PULL MY SWORD OUT! I GUESS YOU STILL HAVE YOUR STRENGTH.
FWSSH
I WON'T FORGIVE YOU FOR THIS! I'LL KILL YOU!
I SAID, GO!

HMPH! WAIT HERE, OLD MAN. I'LL BE BACK AFTER I CAPTURE THE PRINCE.
GRANDPA.
HNGH...
WHA?!
MY BODY?

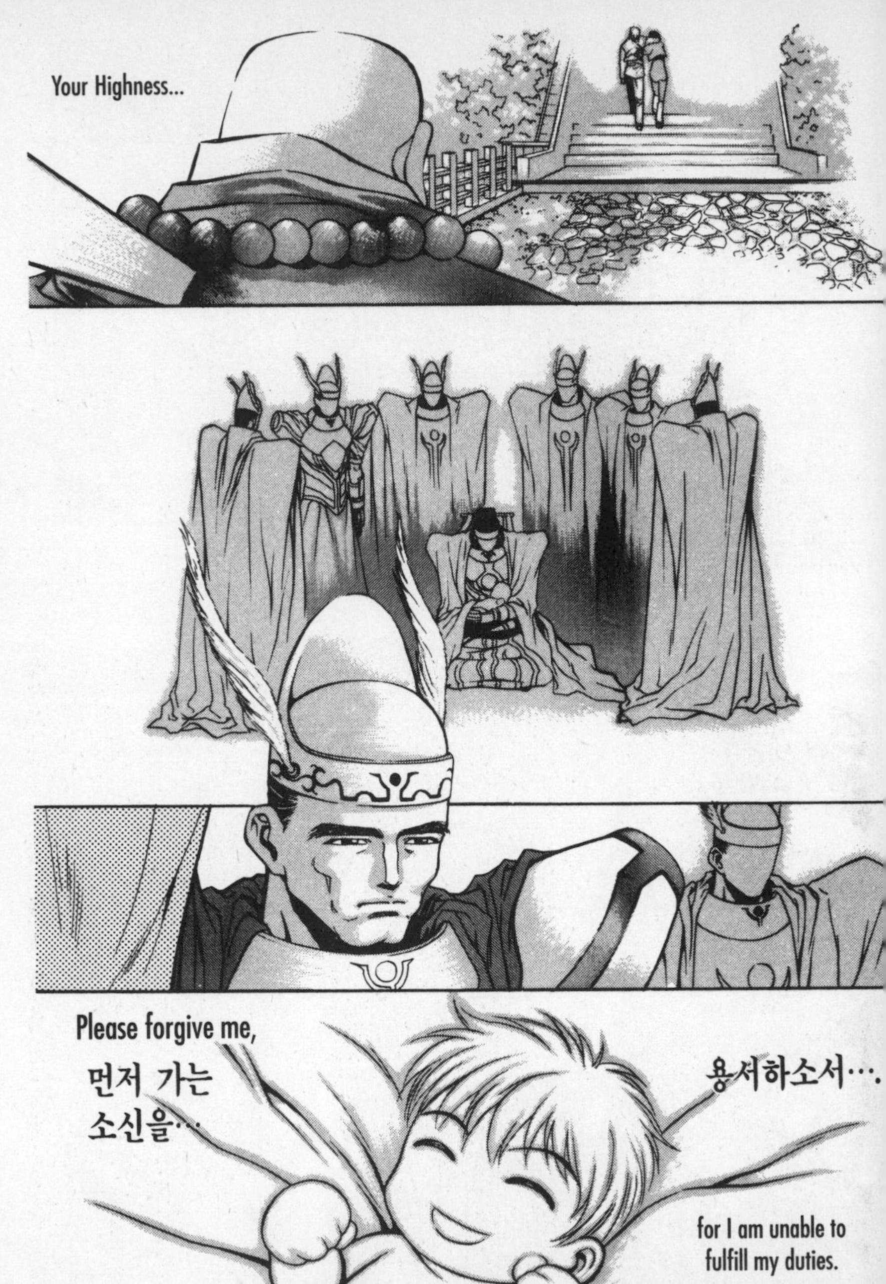
Your Highness...
Please forgive me,
먼저 가는
소신을…
용서하소서….
for I am unable to
fulfill my duties.

무서워마소서…
태자전하.
Please do not
be afraid,
Your Highness.

I'm but a mere
servant, here for
your protection.
소신은 전하를
지키는 종에
불과할 따름입니다.

AAH...

THP
두욱

FIRE!

BWOOF!

GENERAL MARI HAS ARRIVED, YOUR MAJESTY.

YOUR MAJESTY, I'M AFRAID I HAVE BAD NEWS TO REPORT.
AH...

WELCOME, ENERAL MARI.
I'VE DISHONORED YOUR WORTHY NAME, LORD HAE-MO-SOO. I'LL GLADLY RECEIVE ANY PUNISHMENT YOUR MAJESTY SEES FIT.
NO, NO. **I'M** THE ONE AT FAULT HERE.
I SHOULD'VE WENT ABOUT THIS MORE PRUDENTLY.

EVEN FOR AN EXPERIENCED GENERAL LIKE YOURSELF, TAKING ON THE GREAT GENERAL TAI-GONG-WANG **HAD** TO BE DIFFICULT.

I'VE OFFERED A REWARD FOR THE SAFE RETURN OF PRINCE CHI-WOO, SO HE SHOULD SOON BE IN OUR CUSTODY.

YOU MUST BE TIRED. YOU MAY LEAVE NOW.

BAHRON!

HAHA! YOUR MAJESTY IS ALWAYS BENEVOLENT AND KIND.

IT MUST'VE BEEN A TOUGH FIGHT.

THE GREAT GENERAL TAI-GONG-WANG IS NOW DEAD.

I SEE.
THE GREAT GENERAL HAS FINALLY...

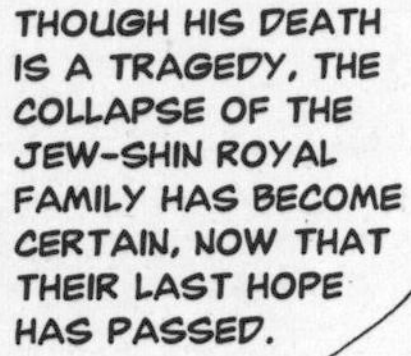
CHANGE OF POWER FROM THE JEW-SHIN FAMILY TO THE BOO-YUH FAMILY IS ONLY A MATTER OF TIME.
THOUGH HIS DEATH IS A TRAGEDY, THE COLLAPSE OF THE JEW-SHIN ROYAL FAMILY HAS BECOME CERTAIN, NOW THAT THEIR LAST HOPE HAS PASSED.

YOU'VE SUCCESSFULLY THWARTED THE INVASION OF THE JOONG-HWA PEOPLE, FOR WHICH YOU'LL BE REMEMBERED AS THE **GREAT HERO** OF THIS LAND. THE WORLD IS NOW YOURS.
THE JEW-SHIN FAMILY, WHO LIVED IN SQUANDER DURING A TIME OF PEACE, HAS LOST THEIR POWER WITH THE SUDDEN DEATHS OF THE EMPER-OR AND THE EMPRESS.

I CONGRATULATE YOU, YOUR MAJESTY!

YOUR MERITS HAVE BEEN THE VIRTUE OF THIS SUCCESS, DUKE BAHRON!

HE WHO HAS BETRAYED ONE IS BOUND TO BETRAY ANOTHER. SUCH MEN ARE **NOT** TO BE TRUSTED.

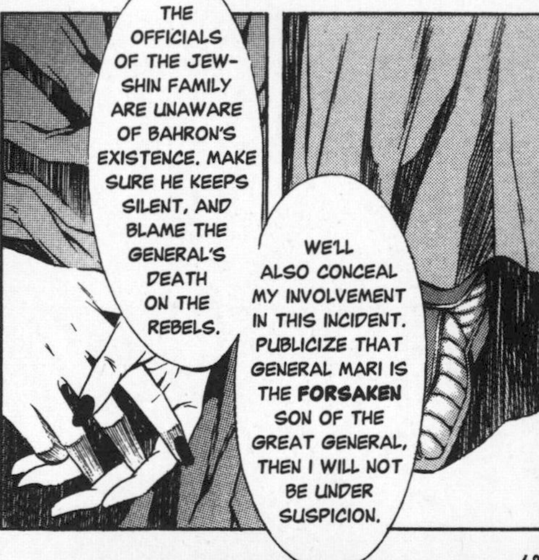

THE OFFICIALS OF THE JEW-SHIN FAMILY ARE UNAWARE OF BAHRON'S EXISTENCE. MAKE SURE HE KEEPS SILENT, AND BLAME THE GENERAL'S DEATH ON THE REBELS.
WE'LL ALSO CONCEAL MY INVOLVEMENT IN THIS INCIDENT. PUBLICIZE THAT GENERAL MARI IS THE **FORSAKEN** SON OF THE GREAT GENERAL, THEN I WILL NOT BE UNDER SUSPICION.

ELIMINATE BAHRON THE ASSASSIN!

THE PRINCE IS THE ONLY ONE LEFT.
DON'T YOU AGREE, ELLEA?

!

ARE YOU UP NOW, YOUR HIGHNESS?

WHAT, WORRIED SOMETHING MIGHT'VE HAPPENED?

Gadirok
REQUIEM CHORUS

ANOTHER STIR-FRIED BEEF FOR TABLE FIVE!
THAT'S THE OWNER'S DAUGHTER?

HEH, I CAN'T BELIEVE SHE'S GROWN SO MUCH.
JUST CHECK OUT THOSE MELONS.
HEH HEH, RIGHT.
SQUISH
SQUISH
KER-BLAM!
WHY DON'T YOU TWO PERVERTS TAKE YOUR FOUL MOUTHS SOMEWHERE ELSE?
YOU LITTLE BRAT!
I'LL KILL YOU!
OH!
FWSSH
STOP RIGHT THERE!
THWACK

BURP
꺼억

GENTLEMEN, YOU'RE NOT ABOUT TO STIR UP **TROUBLE** IN MY INN, ARE YOU?

HE'S BEEN DRINKING IN THE KITCHEN AGAIN.

AHEH. O- OF COURSE NOT.

I KNEW I MISUNDERSTOOD. NOW, WHY DON'T YOU TWO BUY ME A **DRINK**?

DON'T DRINK **TOO** MUCH!

ER...

I FEEL SO BAD FOR BEING A BURDEN, SO I'VE DECIDED TO GO COLLECT SOME OFFERINGS.

OFFERING BAG

MONK GARB

WHERE ARE YOU GOING, LADY SO-AH?

NO NEED TO DO THAT. THERE'RE FAVORS WE OWE TO THE MASTER OURSELVES.
FLAP
IT'S OKAY. I'LL **STEAL** A LOT, SO BE PREPARED TO BE AMAZED!
S-STEAL?

BOY! IT'S GETTIN' CHILLY OUT HERE. LOOKS LIKE WINTER'S-A-COMIN'.
어슬렁
SWAGGER
THWP THWP
Rookie!
Been in the service too long...
STILL HAVEN'T FINISHED YOUR ROUND?
YEAH. HEY, ROOKIE! GO FINISH PUTTIN' UP THE REST OF THEM POSTERS!
YES SIR!
I'LL BE RIGHT WITH YOU. I NEED TO CHECK ON ANOTHER CUSTOMER.
SURE, TAKE YOUR TIME.

DAMN REBELS. WHERE DO THEY FIND THE NERVE TO KIDNAP OUR PRINCE DURING TROUBLED TIMES LIKE THESE?
THE REBELS HAVE KIDNAPPED THE PRINCE FROM THE HOSPITAL WHERE HE WAS STAYING.
WHAT IS IT?

G-GAT!!

HUH?!

MOVE, MOVE.
OUCH, MY NOSE!

HMPH! SO THE **COWARD** HAS COME BACK!
MY **NOSE!**

GAT? ISN'T HE THE ONE RESPONSIBLE FOR ALL THOSE KILLINGS IN THE PAST?
MURMUR
수군
THE SITUATION LOOKS LIKE IT'LL GET WORSE.
수군
MURMUR
끔틀
TWITCH

DIDN'T YOU GUYS HEAR WHAT I JUST **SAID**?! I SAID I'LL **DESTROY** HIM!

I'M TELLING YOU, THAT LITTLE PUNK HAS ALWAYS BEEN SCARED OF ME.
UH, HEY.

WHAT?! WHAT DO **YOU** WANT?!
FWSSSSH

FLINCH
움찔

WHAT THE...? HOW **DARE** HE CALMLY IGNORE ME?!
STOP SHAKING FIRST.

LOOKS LIKE THERE'S GOING TO BE **ANOTHER** ROUND OF KILLINGS. LET'S HURRY AND GET HOME.
SHOULDN'T WE REPORT THIS?
WHY BOTHER? IT'S NOT LIKE ANYONE CAN STOP THEM. IT'S BEST TO KEEP QUIET.

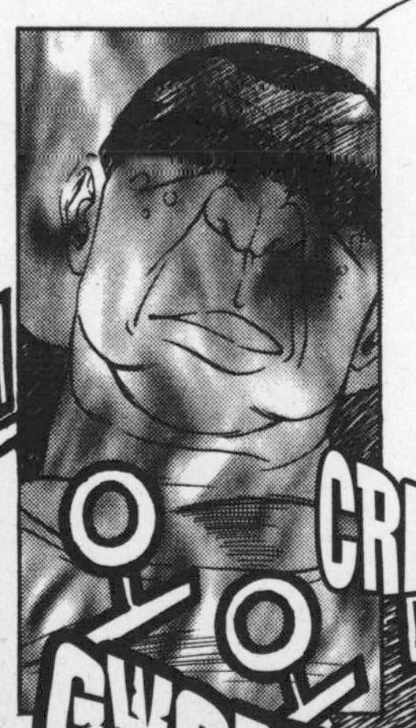
FINALLY, I GET THE CHANCE TO GET REVENGE FOR THIS **SCAR**!
CRKCRK
GWORR

KNOCK KNOCK
EXCUSE ME.

OH MY! YOU HAVEN'T TOUCHED YOUR MEAL.

YOU REALLY SHOULD TRY TO EAT, ESPECIALLY SINCE YOU'RE NOT WELL.

LET ME CLOSE THE WINDOW FOR YOU. WEATHER'S BEEN CHILLY LATELY, AND IT GETS EVEN COLDER AT NIGHT.
VWIIIIING
지
IF YOU HAPPEN TO CATCH A COLD...
THEN I WON'T BE ABLE TO LOOK LADY SO-AH IN THE EYES.

Cover yourself with this, Your Highness.
It's okay.

Please, Your Highness. If you happen to get ill, then I won't be able to look His Majesty in the eyes.

ELLEA?

WOW, YOU **SPOKE**! SO YOU CAN TALK, AFTER ALL! I THOUGHT YOU **LOST** YOUR ABILITY TO SPEAK!

ANYWAY... WHO'S ELLEA?

YOU HAVE SUCH A NICE VOICE. YOU REALLY SHOULDN'T HIDE IT.

YES! DRINK AS MUCH AS YOU WANT! IT'S **ALL** ON ME!

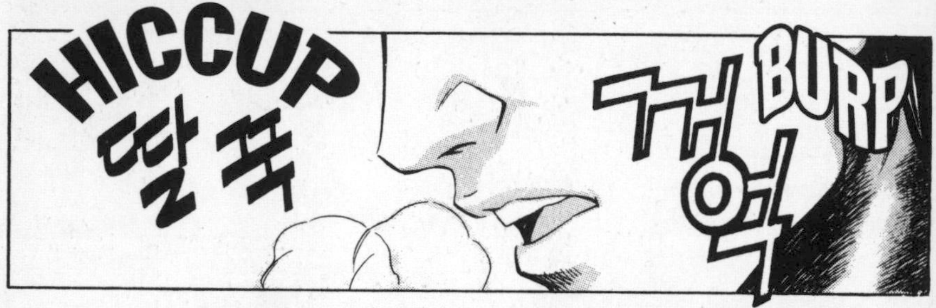

HAHA, **DUKE** BAHRON...

HAHAHA! I LIKE IT! NOW I CAN FINALLY HAVE A TERRITORY OF MY **OWN**!

I AM **DUKE** BAHRON!
EVERYONE! BOW YOUR HEADS, AND HEED THE **DUKE'S** ORDERS!

EH? WHO THE HELL ARE YOU? A SOLDIER FOR THE JEW-SHIN FAMILY?

!

Y-YOU ARE!

ELLEA!

IT **CAN'T** BE! YOU SHOULD BE **DEAD**!

Historical aspects of *Gadirok*...(1)

Taigongwang Lu Shang

He is a real historical figure named Lu Shang (also known as Jiang Ziya or Jiang Shang). When the Shin-Jew-Shin* Empire, an empire which served the Dong-Yi tribe*, declared Gae-Ah-Ji-Jew-Shin its vassal country, it caused the Shin-Jew-Shin Empire to lose a lot of its strength. Lu Shang realized that the Emperor would not be able to focus on the well-being of his people, so he formed a group of soldiers and led them in hopes of declaring independence from the Shin-Jew-Shin Empire. However, the continuous invasions of the neighboring countries, particularly the Yin Dynasty and Shang Dynasty, were too much for Lu Shang and his soldiers. As a result, Lu Shang had to give up his hopes of independence. Extremely disappointed, he wrote the first-ever book on militaristic strategies, Liutao (Six Strategies), and regressed into a life of a fisherman. However, the real purpose of his regression was to wait for the right opportunity and the right Emperor for him to assist. One day, the Emperor of Zhou Dynasty came across Lu Shang, and after a short conversation with Lu Shang, he realized this was not an ordinary man and asked Lu Shang for assistance in governing his dynasty. Lu Shang accepted and went with the Emperor of Zhou Dynasty, eventually playing a major part in Zhou Dynasty conquering the Yin Dynasty. He was seventy at the time. The feat was obviously impossible without Lu Shang, and these facts are written in Chinese history...

-An excerpt taken from a book published by Dr. San-Ho Kim, titled Dae-Jew-Shin-Jeh-Gook-Sah. (The Historical Facts of the Great Jew-Shin Empire)

*The word "Jew-Shin" later became "Cho-Sun," which is a word used when referring to the ancient Koreans.

*Dong-Yi tribe is considered as the ancestors of the people of Korea. The word "Dong-Yi" stands for "Men of virtue who use the giant bow of the East." Many historical records indicate that Jiang Tai Gong is actually from the Dong-Yi tribe.

The Great General Tai-Gong-Wang

He is the captain of the Royal Guards of Emperor Sa-Wa-Ra, Prince Chi-Woo's father. Assisting the Emperor, he has won many battles fighting alongside the Emperor. He's also a person who has had tremendous influence on Prince Chi-Woo's militaristic knowledge, as well as mental strength. After the One Year War, the last battle led by Emperor Sa-Wa-Ra, he leaves his position as the Captain of the Royal Guards and settles down deep in the mountains, eventually becoming a Buddhist monk. The reason behind his sudden departure is only known to the Emperor and the Great General himself. (Involves the secret behind the birth of Prince Chi-Woo). He is the main character that will help unravel the storyline of this book.

*This character was created based on the historical figure above, as well as other characters in this book (e.g., Prince Chi-Woo, Emperor Sa-Wa-Ra, etc). THE STORIES BEHIND THESE CHARACTERS ARE NOT THE ACTUAL STORIES BEHIND THE HISTORICAL FIGURES WHICH THE CHARACTERS HAVE BEEN MODELED AFTER.

Gadirok
REQUIEM CHORUS
GADIROK
5520

YOU'RE SUPPOSED TO BE DEAD.
I COULD'VE SWORN... BY THE HANDS OF THE PRINCE...

I DON'T BELIEVE MY EYES.
DID YOU COME BACK TO GET ME? IS **THAT** IT?

H-HEY. IT **HAS** TO BE A MISTAKE. I STILL HAVE THINGS TO DO IN THIS REALM.

DAMN IT!

N-NO...
I CAN'T DIE LIKE THIS.
I JUST CAN'T.

Hae-Mo-Soo?!
You deceitful bastard!
How could you?!
How foolish of me to believe at least YOU wouldn't treat me like trash.
C...CAVALRYMEN!
기… 기사단!!
Prince Chi-Woo?!

HAHAHA
그래. 그랬군.
그래도 그중 단 한사람.
날 인간취급 해준 자가
있긴 있었군.
Yeah. In the middle of it all, there was only ONE person who'd treated me with respect.
Damn it. I know it's pointless to say this now, but…
젠장.
이제 와서 이런 말 해봤자
아무 소용도 없겠지만…
그래도…
95
I truly apologize, Prince Chi-Woo…Your Highness.

CRKCRKCRK

STOP SHOVING FOOD IN YOUR MOUTH AND ANSWER ME!!
KER-BLAAAM!!
DO YOU HEAR ME NOW, YOU PIECE OF CRAP?!

PAY FOR THE MEAL, FAT BOY!

YOU'VE GOT THE NERVE TO IGNORE ME, AFTER SCREWING UP MY NOSE AND RUNNING AWAY LIKE A LITTLE **COWARD**?!

HEY, UH...

DO I KNOW YOU?

VWORRR

SEE?

I TOLD YOU HE WOULDN'T REMEMBER YOU.

I-IT REALLY **IS** HIM. GAT, THE REBEL WHO KIDNAPPED THE PRINCE!
THIS COULD BE MY CHANCE FOR PROMOTION.

HEY, ROOKIE!
FLINCH

SERGEANT LEE...!
WILL YOU SHUT UP, IDIOT?!

I WANT YOU TO STAY QUIET AND LISTEN TO ME.
I'M SURE YOU COULD USE A VACATION, RIGHT?

NOW, WHAT I WANT YOU TO DO IS SLIP OUT QUIETLY AND REQUEST BACK-UP, WHILE I STAY HERE AND WATCH HIM.
WE COULD RECEIVE **MEDALS** FOR THIS, GOT IT?

쾅
SLAM

FWSSH

EAT **THIS**! I HOPE YOU HAVE NOTHING BUT **BAD LUCK** FOR THE REST OF YOUR LIFE!

빠샤

I'D RATHER STARVE TO DEATH THAN BEG FOR YOUR HELP!
HMPH! I WANTED TO COLLECT OFFERINGS THE WAY I'D BEEN TAUGHT,
BUT, FROM NOW ON, I'LL DO IT MY WAY.
WELL, SO MUCH
FOR THAT...

WOW! A GARION!
THE ANIMAL THAT ONLY THE NOBLES CAN RIDE...

Emperor Chi-Woo (In Chinese, the name is pronounced "Chi-You")

He is known as the Emperor Chi-Woo The Great, the fourteenth emperor of The Bae Dal Empire. Regarded as the greatest and the bravest emperor in Korean history, the entire eastern and northern part of China, along with the Korean peninsula, were once under his control (More specifically Huai-Nan, Shan-Dong, Beijing, among others, of China). The people of Emperor Chi-Woo, collectively known as the Dong-Yi tribe, were constantly in battle with the Hua-Shan tribe, the native tribe of the land which later became China. Emperor Chi-Woo and the Hua-Shan tribe were involved in more than seventy battles, all of which were decisively won by Emperor Chi-Woo. The Hua-Shan tribe acknowledged Emperor Chi-Woo's brilliance in militaristic knowledge, and built shrines in their territories, dedicated to the emperor. Eventually, the battle ended with the Hua-Shan tribe on the losing end. However, Emperor Chi-Woo granted lordship to the leader of the Hua-Shan tribe, and allowed the Hua-Shan tribe to settle in their territories.

Emperor Chi-Woo was known for carrying around his bronze helmet by placing it on the horn of a cow, which caused the Hua-Shan tribe to actually believe that Emperor Chi-Woo had horns on his head. The general impression of Emperor Chi-Woo among Chinese people is rather intimidating, almost portraying him as a supernatural figure, such as a goblin or a ghost. From the general impressions alone, you can tell just how much of an intimidating figure the Emperor really was, and still is, to the Chinese.

-An excerpt taken from a book published by Dr. San-Ho Kim, titled Dae-Jew-Shin-Jeh-Gook-Sah ("The Historical Facts of the Great Jew-Shin Empire").

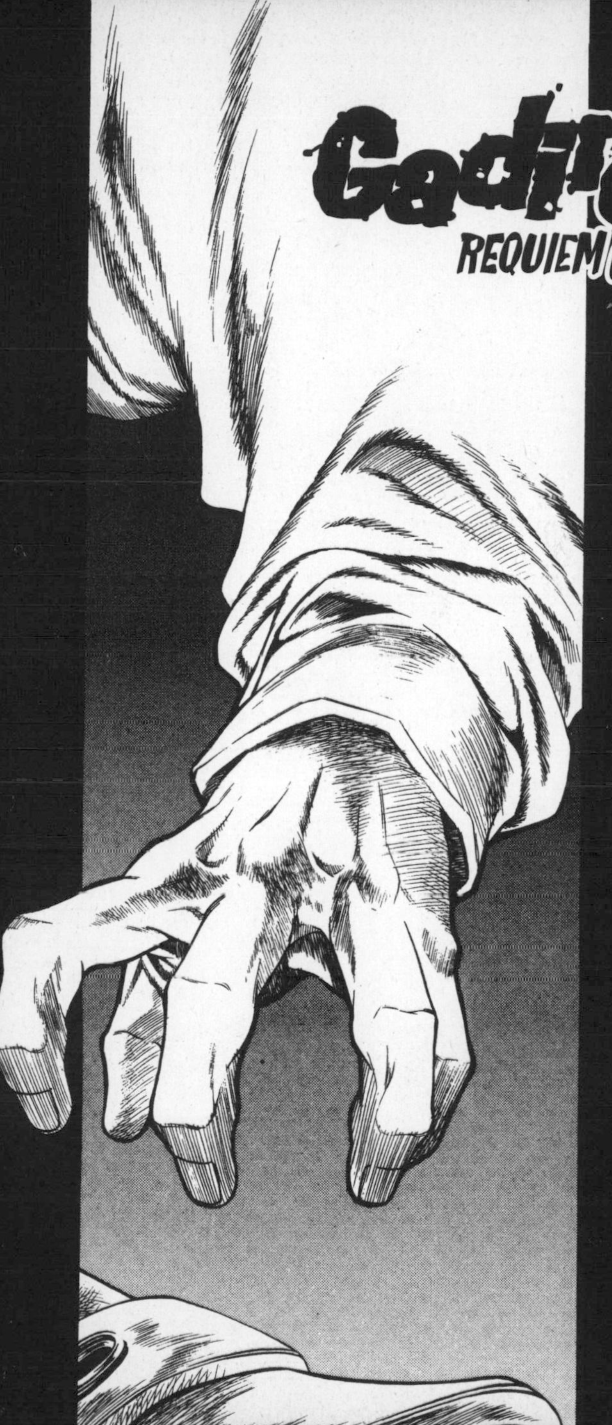
Gadirok
REQUIEM CHORUS

WHY IS IT SO NOISY DOWNSTAIRS?

I BETTER GO. I'VE BEEN GONE FOR TOO LONG.

LET ME KNOW IF YOU NEED ANY-THING.

CREEAK
끼이익

쾅
SLAM
DANGER...!
WHAT'S GOING ON? WHAT'S ALL THE COMMOTION ABOUT?
A LOCAL PUNK AND A MYSTERIOUS SWORDSMAN GOT INTO IT A MOMENT AGO.
A MYSTERIOUS SWORDSMAN?

THIS IS DRIVIN' ME **CRAZY**!

THWACK

I SWEAR, THE MILITARY NOWADAYS LACKS DISCIPLINE.

ARE THEY BUILDING AN ARMY?

!

ARE YOU THE ONE WHO REQUESTED BACK-UP?

Y-YES, MY LORD!

WHERE IS HE?

WELL... HE WAS HERE A MOMENT AGO, BUT HE LEFT AFTER AN ARGUMENT WITH A LOCAL PUNK.

BUT, I'M SURE HE DIDN'T GET FAR. AND, IF HE'S HERE, THEN THAT SHOULD MEAN THE LITTLE GIRL'S HERE, ALSO.
A GREAT CHANCE FOR US TO GET RID OF THE REBELS AND RESCUE THE PRINCE, MY LORD.

LITTLE GIRL?

ARE YOU TALKING ABOUT **THIS** LITTLE GIRL?

HEY, MOLE FACE! I SAID UNTIE ME AND FIGHT ME! WHAT, ARE YOU **SCARED**?!

화악

FWSSH!

MY LORD, YOU TRULY ARE REMARKABLE.
LADY SO-AH!

MISS YERINA!

WELL, LOOK WHO IT IS. I DIDN'T EXPECT TO FIND **YOU** HERE. I GUESS IT'S A SMALL WORLD, AFTER ALL.

WHAT HAPPENED? I THOUGHT YOU WERE COLLECTING OFFERINGS.
WELL...

SEARCH THIS PLACE! THEY MIGHT HAVE ACCOMPLICES! FIND ANY AND ALL INCRIMINATING EVIDENCE RELATED TO THE REBELS' HIDING PLACE!

GASP

DO NOT WORRY ABOUT THE INN! FROM NOW ON, THIS PROPERTY BELONGS TO **ME**, DUKE GEH-RU!

TURN THIS PLACE INSIDE OUT!
AAAH!

KILL ANYONE WHO INTERFERES!

W-WHAT ARE YOU TALKING ABOUT? THIS IS A LEGITIMATE ESTABLISHMENT—MY FATHER LEGALLY OBTAINED AND OPERATED IT FOR OVER **TEN** YEARS!

YOUR PUNISHMENT FOR ASSISTING THE PRINCE'S KIDNAPPERS IS...

DEATH!

YOU BASTARD! MISS YERINA HAD NOTHING TO DO WITH IT!

LET GO OF ME, YOU COWARDS!
YOU LITTLE BRAT! HOW DARE YOU OPEN YOUR MOUTH?!
FWAP

BUT, SINCE WE ARE ACQUAIN-TANCES, I'LL SPARE YOUR LIFE FOR ONE NIGHT...
IN MY ROOM, THAT IS.

DON'T YOU WANT TO SHOW GAT OUR SPECIAL RELATIONSHIP?

GAT?!
H-HE'S HERE?!

THE BOY WILL RETURN TO THE TEMPLE TO CONTACT THE GIRL! STATION OUR SEARCH CREWS AND SPECIAL FORCES WITHIN **ONE** KILOMETER OF THIS INN!
YES, MY LORD!
MY LORD! I FOUND THIS MAN SITTING IN THE GIRL'S ROOM!
IT SEEMS LIKE HE'S NOT IN A RIGHT STATE OF MIND.

HOW FAR ARE WE GOING?

WE'RE HERE. THIS PLACE WILL SOON BE YOUR GRAVE.

WHY DID YOU BRING ME HERE?
YOU WERE THE COWARD.
STOP PRETENDING YOU DON'T REMEMBER! THIS IS WHERE YOU SCREWED-UP MY NOSE!
AHEM!
I'LL TELL YOU.
I DIDN'T WANNA TALK ABOUT IT, BUT SINCE YOU DON'T SEEM TO REMEMBER,
?
SEE? YOU WERE THE COWARD.

HEY, THIS ISN'T THE TIME.

I KNOW! STOP BUGGING ME!

SHP

DAMN IT. I WISH I COULD CRUSH YOU RIGHT HERE, BUT SINCE THERE'S SOMEONE ELSE WANTING TO SEE YOU, I'LL JUST HAVE TO WAIT.

IT'S BEEN A LONG TIME, **BOSS**!

SHI-WOOL, YOU...
HEY, BOSS... I MEAN, GAT!

HOW DARE YOU COME BACK, AND AS A FELON AT THAT, AFTER YOU RAN OFF USING YERINA AS BAIT?
WHAT ARE YOU PLANNING TO DO TO HER **THIS** TIME?

Yerina!!

YOU IGNORANT FOOL! LOWER THAT SWORD AWAY FROM OUR PRINCE!

H-HE'S THE PRINCE?!

FLINCH
"OUR PRINCE?"

HE'S PRINCE CHI-WOO?!

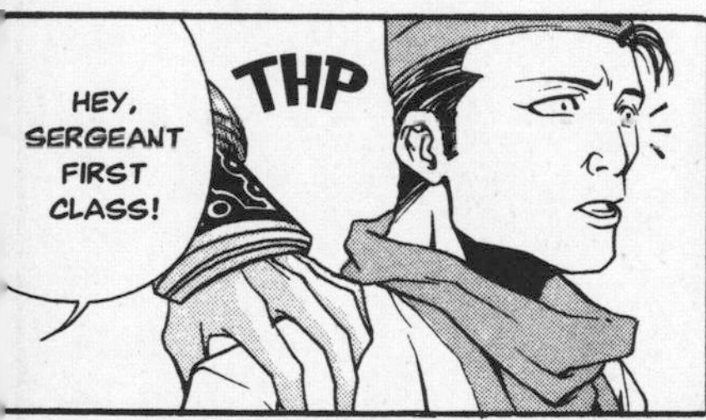
HEY, SERGEANT FIRST CLASS!
THP

I CONGRATULATE YOU ON YOUR PROMOTION.

M-MY LORD? I'M STILL A SERGEANT.

YOUR HIGHNESS.
I HAD THE HONOR OF MEETING YOUR HIGHNESS ONCE. I WISH YOU PROSPERITY.

Gadirok

REQUIEM CHORUS

YOU MEAN, SHE'S HERE?
YERINA!

WHEN DID SHE RETURN? IS SHE ALL RIGHT?

YOU'RE NOT FOOLING ANYONE, GAT.
YOU CAME BACK BECAUSE YOU KNEW SHE WAS HERE! I KNOW YOU CAME BACK TO USE HER AGAIN, TO EXTEND THAT SORRY LIFE OF YOURS A LITTLE LONGER!

WHERE WERE YOU WHEN SHE WAS CRYING? AREN'T YOU THE TYPE OF PERSON WHO ABANDONS PEOPLE AFTER THEY LOSE THEIR USEFULNESS?

I ASKED YOU A QUESTION!

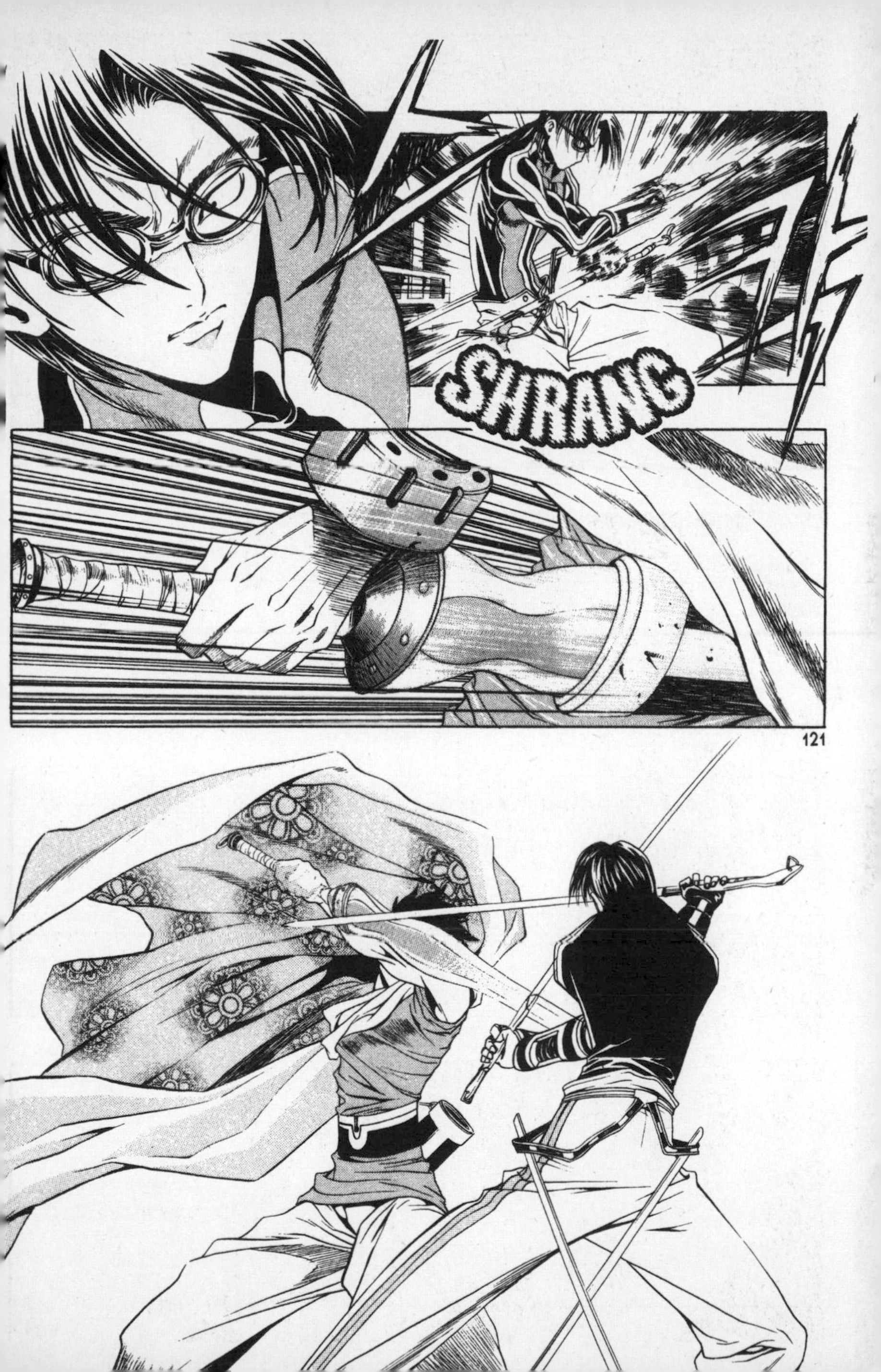
SHRANG

YOU DON'T HAVE THE **RIGHT** TO ASK SUCH QUESTIONS.

DON'T TRY ANYTHING. JUST ACT NORMAL.

201

CREAK

I SEE YOU'VE BEEN THROUGH A LOT, YOUR HIGHNESS.

WE SHALL CELEBRATE AS SOON AS WE CATCH THE REBELS.
TNK

THIS MAY NOT BE FITTING FOR YOUR HIGHNESS, BUT I WISH TO SERVE YOU MY MOST TREASURED LIQUOR...
GLUB GLUB
THIS IS AN IMPORTED LIQUOR FROM THE WEST CALLED **RED WINE**. LIKE ITS COLOR, IT HAS A RICH TASTE THAT'S ABSOLUTELY ASTOUNDING.

BURBLE
BURBLE

SPLSSH
AAARGH!!

AHHHH!!

THUMP

SHATTER

PFT!

PWAHAHA!!

IT REALLY **IS** TRUE. THE PRINCE HAS INDEED BECOME A **BASKET CASE!**

TO SEE THE ONCE ARROGANT PRINCE INSANE...
THE RUMOR ABOUT THE WORLD NOW BELONGING TO GENERAL HAE-MO-SOO IS TRUE AFTER ALL
BURBLE BURBLE
부글 부글
GIVE US BACK...
OUR LIVES AND
OUR BODIES...
THERE ISN'T ANYTHING I CAN DO, SO PLEASE LEAVE ME ALONE.

HEY, PRINCE! WHEN ARE YOU GOING TO STOP ACTING LIKE A **NUT**?

GET UP AND DRINK. WHAT, ARE YOU TOO **GOOD** TO ACCEPT A DRINK FROM A DUKE?

FINE, THEN HOW ABOUT YOU LICK THE WINE OFF OF YOUR "EXALTED" BODY?

AAAAAH!
PWAHAHA! JUST **LOOK** AT THAT IDIOT!

AAAAH!!

FWOOOSH
SHATTER

후두둑
THPTHPTHP

WHAT'S HAPPENED TO YOU, SHI-WOOL? I DON'T UNDERSTAND WHY A GENTLE SOUL LIKE YOU IS ACTING THIS WAY.
TELL ME! I'LL BE FORCED TO CONSIDER YOU AN **ENEMY** IF YOU DON'T HAVE A VALID REASON.

I USED TO ADMIRE YOU. NO, I **WORSHIPPED** YOU.
하악 하아
HUFF HUFF
I EVEN GAVE UP ON YERINA BECAUSE OF MY OBSESSIVE DESIRE TO BE JUST **LIKE** YOU.
I TOLD MYSELF, EVEN IF SHE'S UNHAPPY, IT'S OKAY.
SHE WAS WITH **YOU**, AND THAT'S ALL THAT MATTERED.

BUT YOU SHOULDN'T HAVE MADE HER MISERABLE!

ARE YOU REFERRING TO HER HAVING BEEN SOLD AS A SERVANT IN MY PLACE?

YEAH, SHE WAS TAKEN AWAY! RIGHT AFTER THE DUKE HAD BOUGHT YOU...

SHE WAS AFRAID THE DUKE MIGHT ATTEMPT TO HARM YOU AFTER WHAT YOU'D DONE TO HIS SON, SO **SHE** CHOSE TO GO IN YOUR PLACE.
DID YOU KNOW THAT?!

I DIDN'T KNOW IT THEN. SHE TOLD ME TO BE IN HIDING UNTIL SHE SMOOTHED THINGS OVER WITH SOME MONEY. SO I THOUGHT...

ARE YOU EVEN AWARE OF THE PAIN SHE HAS SUFFERED?! THE HUMILIATION SHE HAD TO ENDURE?!

God Rok
REQUIEM CHORUS

WHAT HAPPENED TO YOUR EYE?
I'D TRIED TO TAKE YOUR PLACE.
UNFORTUNATELY, THINGS DIDN'T QUITE TURN OUT AS I EXPECTED...

YOUR EYE.

I'D AMBUSHED THE DUKE, ON HIS WAY BACK FROM A HUNTING TRIP.
사냥을 마치고 돌아가던 성주를 습격했었다.

THOUGH MY SKILLS WEREN'T QUITE ADEQUATE ENOUGH TO TAKE HIS LIFE,
내 실력으론 나의 한쪽 눈과 성주의 목숨을 바꾸는 건 무리였어.

그래도 중상을 입은 성주는 자신의 자리를 장남에게 내어주더군.
I'D WOUNDED THE DUKE ENOUGH TO FORCE BESTOWING OF ALL POWERS TO HIS ELDEST SON...
TO GEH-RU, THE ONE WHOM YOU'D ALMOST KILLED.
너에게 죽을 뻔했던 그 게루 놈에게 말야.

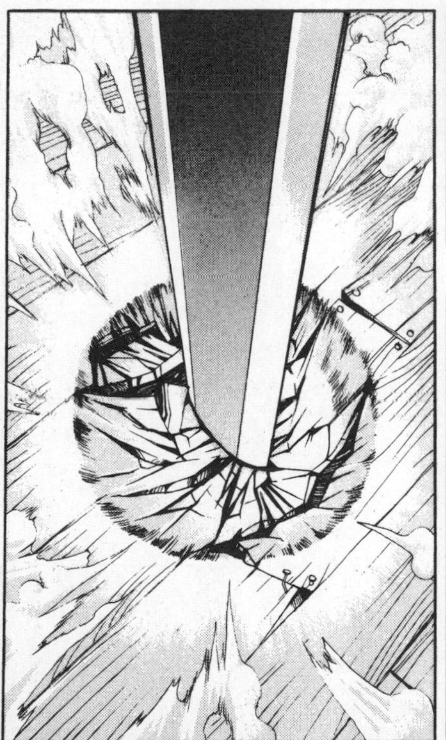

Inner energy? No, it feels different...

FWSSH
SHWSSSH
138
FWOOOM

WHAT THE?!
HOW DID THE
SOLDIERS...?!

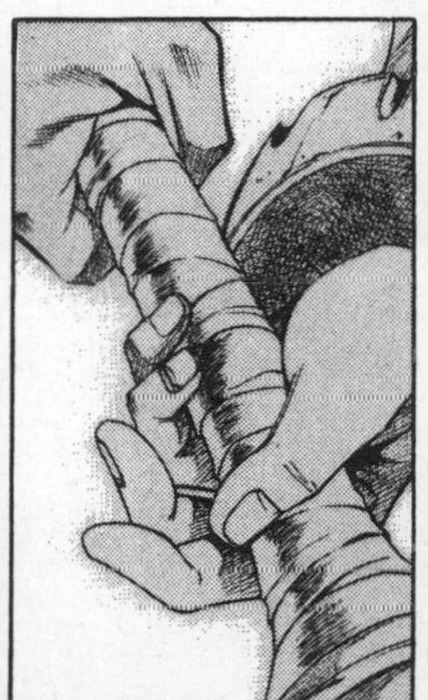

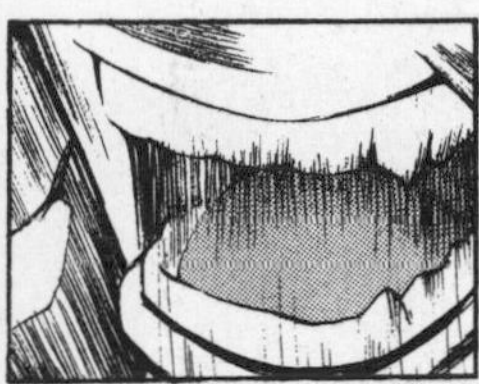

THWUMP

Unbelievable!

FOURTH BATTALION! STAND BY!

HOLY CRAP! WHAT WAS I THINKING, PROVOKING **HIM**?

SMACK
FWSH

OH, RIGHT!

KRACK

YOU'VE CHANGED, GAT.
WHAT MADE YOU LIKE THIS? JUST WHAT KIND OF LIFE DID YOU...

BOSS! I'VE BEEN TOLD THE DUKE HAS TAKEN OVER MISS YERINA'S INN AND HAS THE PRINCE IN CUSTODY!

WHAT ABOUT YERINA?! WHAT ABOUT HER AGONIES?!
IT'S HIM, THE MAN WHO CHANGED ME. I HAVE TO FIND HIM.

ACCEPTING THE WORLD AS IT IS MEANT FORGETTING ABOUT MYSELF.

I WILL DEDICATE MY LIFE TO GAINING ATONEMENT FOR HER SUFFERING.
MY LIFE...
RIGHT NOW, I HAVE TO SAVE HIM.
HE EXISTS— THEREFORE, I EXIST.
MY LIFE ENDURES **AFTER** HIS.

AAAH! NOW THIS IS GOOD WINE!

I'M ANXIOUSLY AWAITING GAT, MY TICKET TO FAME AND GLORY!

AAAAAH!
THMP
쿵
AAAAAAH!
쿵
THMP
쿵
THMP

THMP
THMP
LET ME OUT! I'M SCARED!!
OPEN THE DOOR! HURRY!
THMP
THMP
THMP
What's causing you so much pain, Your Highness?
What is bothering you so much?

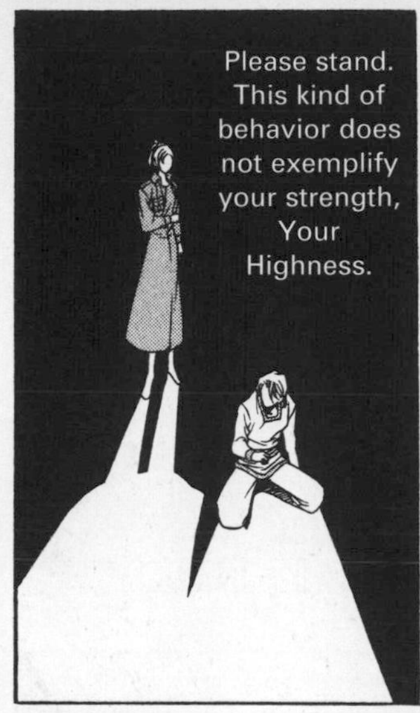
Please stand. This kind of behavior does not exemplify your strength, Your Highness.

Help me, Ellea. Get me out of here!

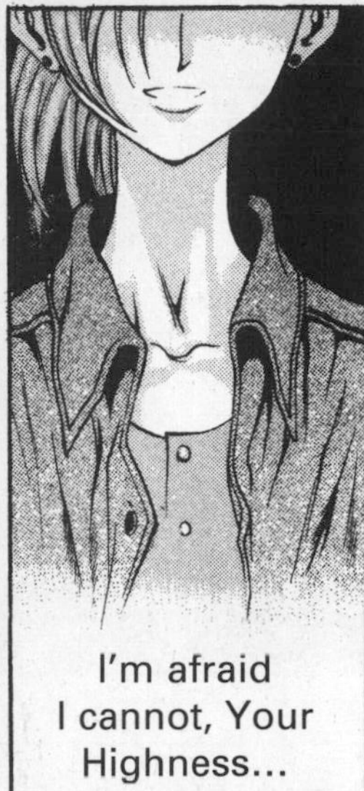
I'm afraid I cannot, Your Highness...

for I am **dead**.

Everyone died.

For whom did they sacrifice their lives?

COULD IT BE FOR ME?

HE'S HERE!

THWUMP
FWSSSSH

Gadirok
REQUIEM CHORUS

I HEAR THE WORLD IS IN TURMOIL THESE DAYS.

IT BEGAN WITH THE ESCAPE OF THE PRINCE.
MY PLAN OF USING THE PRINCE AS BAIT TO ELIMINATE ALL JEW-SHIN OFFICIALS HAS FAILED, DUE TO THEIR SWIFT ACTIONS.
ALSO, I'M BEGINNING TO NOTICE THE MOVEMENTS OF JEW-SHIN OFFICIALS, WHOM WE'D DRIVEN OUT INTO THE SUBURBS.
IF THEY GET TO THE PRINCE FIRST, THINGS ARE GOING TO GET OUT OF CONTROL.
SHP
I'VE BEEN INFORMED THAT A DUKE HAS THE PRINCE IN CUSTODY.
THWP
THWP

SHWAAACK

I WANT YOU TO GO THERE, ELLEA!

후우
WHEW

TH-THUMP
쿵
쿵

KILL THE PRINCE ALONG WITH THE REBELS!

I'LL SEND THE TROOPS FIRST THING IN THE MORNING. TAKE CARE OF EVERYTHING BEFORE THEY ARRIVE.
FIRST, TAKE CARE OF THE REBELS SO WE CAN BLAME THEM FOR THE MURDER OF THE PRINCE.
PURGING OF THE JEW-SHIN OFFICIALS WILL COMMENCE AFTERWARDS.
TRY TO BE COURTEOUS, FOR HE WAS ONCE YOUR LOVER.

KER-KRACK

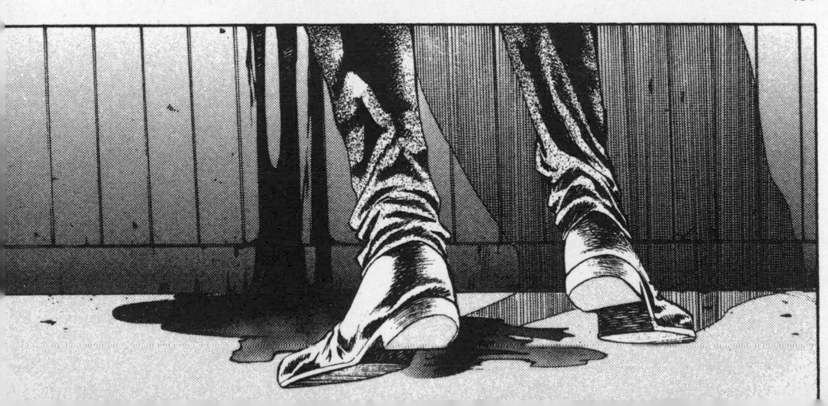

YOU AREN'T FOOLING ANYONE.

YAHI

ARE YOU PROUD OF BEING SOLDIERS?

THEN STOP ACTING **COWARDLY** AND PICK UP YOUR SWORDS.

DAMN, HE **KNOWS**! EVERYONE, IN YOUR ATTACK POSITIONS!

GOOD. THAT'S HOW HAE-MO-SOO'S **SERVANTS** ARE SUPPOSED TO BEHAVE.
HMPH!
YOU BASTARD! HOW DARE YOU **RIDICULE** THE SOLDIERS OF HIS MAJESTY?!
SHRANG
SERVANTS WHO DO NOT RECOGNIZE THE CHANGE OF THEIR MASTERS ARE WORSE THAN DOGS.
WHAT?!
FIRE!

KA-BOOM

BLRRGH!
AAAAH!

DO NOT PANIC! HOLD YOUR POSITIONS AND STAY ALERT!

I SEE YOU KNOW HOW TO USE SPELLS, BUT IT'S USELESS AGAINST ME!
I'VE GRADUATED WITH HONORS FROM THE MILITARY ACADEMY!

SKLRRRSH

COMMANDER!

H-HOW CAN THIS BE?! WE'RE GETTING BUTCHERED BY ONE MAN.

THP
AAAAH!

I CAN'T DIE HERE. I'M GETTING PROMOTED TOMORROW!

HUH?!

THWUMP

Gat...

Why must I always cry behind you?

Stop crying, stupid!

But I can't help it.

Though I've seen you participate in many fights since we were kids, I still cannot get used to it.

The sadness embedded in your never-ending battles,
or your movements that disguise tears and even your most agonizing cries…

I won't even cry in front of you anymore,

for I have no **right** to show such emotions.

THPP

HEH HEH...
WHAT DO YOU SAY WE **CONSUMMATE** OUR RELATIONSHIP, NOW THAT THE MAN-OF-THE-HOUR'S HERE?

Emperor Hae-Mo-Soo

(in Chinese, the name is pronounced "Tian-Wang-Lang Xie-Mu-Shu")

Near the end of the Great Jew-Shin Empire was a time of perpetual turmoil. The old and weakened Jew-Shin Empire was constantly being invaded by neighboring countries. Especially in the Southern region of the Empire, the battle between the Jew-Shin Empire and the tribe who was residing in the region (now known as Zhong Yuan region of China) began to get more and more violent. Also, the generals of the many collapsed empires around the Jew-Shin Empire became bandits and began invading the Jew-Shin Empire. General Hae-Mo-Soo, then twenty three years old, was sent to the Western and Southern part of the region (now known as the Korean peninsula) as the leader of the expeditionary force. Eventually, the territory of the Bool-Jew-Shin Empire, which was still under the control of the Jew-Shin Empire at the time, became his. After gaining the territory, he built a palace on Woong-Shim Mountain to celebrate his accomplishments (In Chinese, the name of the mountain is pronounced "Xiong Xin Mountain").

While General Hae-Mo-Soo was ensuring the safety of the people of the Jew-Shin Empire in the Western region, the Emperor of Jew-Shin threw away his position as emperor and hid in a mountain. Foreseeing the oncoming danger and instability for the people of Jew-Shin, he declared himself emperor in 238 B.C., the birth of the Book-Boo-Yuh Dynasty (In Chinese, the name is pronounced "Bei-Fu-Yu," which later became "Ko-Gu-Ryo"—one of the three dynasties in the beginning of Korea).

When the original emperor of the Jew-Shin Empire didn't return for more than six years after the General Hae-Mo-Soo's declaration, General Hae-Mo-Soo went to Baek-Ak Mountain (A well-known mountain in Korea), where the original emperor of the Jew-Shin Empire and his officials were hiding with a large number of troops. Terrified, the original emperor of the Jew-Shin Empire and his officials decided to formally relinquish the emperor position to General Hae-Mo-Soo. After his emperorship was formally recognized, Emperor Hae-Mo-Soo began his emperorship by taking a census of the people in the empire. In 220 B.C., as a celebration of his attainment of the emperorship, he held a large religious service at the top of Baek-Ak Mountain and had his people build a new palace with three hundred and thirty-six chambers. When it was finished, he named it the Chun-An Palace (In Chinese, the name is pronounced the Tian An Palace, which means "The Palace of Heavenly Peace").
-An excerpt taken from a book published by Dr. San-Ho Kim, titled Dae-Jew-Shin-Jeh-Gook-Sah ("The Historical Facts of the Great Jew-Shin Empire").

Gadirok
REQUIEM CHORUS

GRRROWL
꼬르륵
...

SHP
HUNGRY--

THMP
쾅
THMP
쾅
HEY! ARE YOU TRYING TO STARVE ME TO DEATH?!

WHA?!
SHPLACK

THMP
SIGH...

PSH! THOSE BASTARDS COULD AT LEAST **FEED** ME.

YOU'RE NOT THE **ONLY** ONE STARVING, SO SHUT UP!
Y-YES, SIR.

I HATE HIM. I REALLY HATE HIM...

WHAT KIND OF A MONK PASSES AWAY WITHOUT FULFILLING HIS RESPONSIBILITIES?

You must protect His Highness at all costs! We cannot afford to lose the only hope of this land.

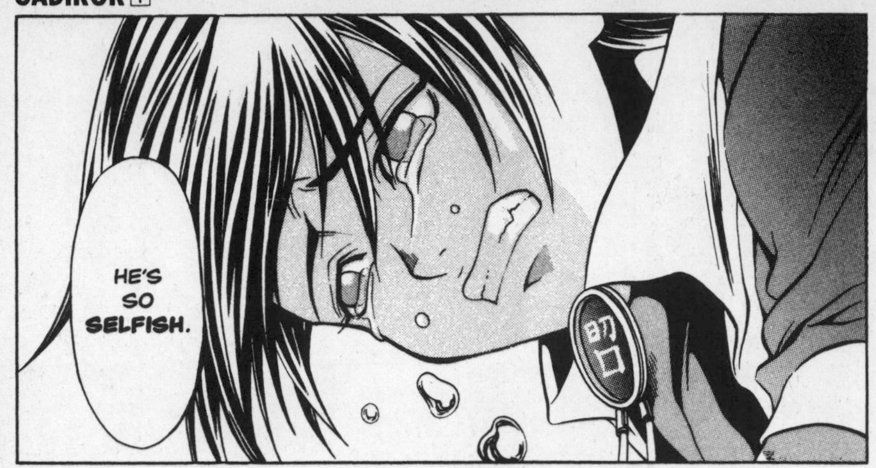
HE'S SO SELFISH.

GRANDPA, WHAT AM I SUPPOSED TO DO NOW...?

THP THP

WE'LL GO THIS WAY. THE REST OF YOU, TAKE CARE OF THE REAR ENTRANCE.
HUH?

EH?

HEY, LOOK! THERE'S SOMEONE LOCKED UP IN THERE!
WHAT?

DAMN! HE'S NOT HUMAN!
THERE'S NO WAY WE CAN WIN. HE'S JUST TOO STRONG.
IT FEELS AS IF...

WE'RE NOTHING BUT A BUNCH OF MICE GOING AGAINST A TIGER!

ker-CLANK
챙
챙
강
L-LET'S GET OUT OF HERE!
I DON'T WANT TO **DIE**!
STOP! ANYONE WHO RUNS WILL BE **EXECUTED**!
DAMN IT. I WANT TO RUN, TOO.

TSK, TSK. **THIS** IS WHY PEASANTS WILL ALWAYS BE PEASANTS.

AN EMOTIONAL REUNION, ISN'T IT? AREN'T YOU GETTING TEARY-EYED?

GET YOUR HANDS **OFF** OF HER!

HEY! DO IT **NOW**!!

SHKRA-KRACK

WHAT'S THIS?

NO, NO! I SUGGEST YOU DO NOT ACT HASTILY.

MY SORCERERS HAVE FORMED A BARRIER AROUND YOU--

LET'S JUST SAY IT'LL BE VERY PAINFUL IF YOU MOVE.

YOU JUST SIT TIGHT AND WATCH YERINA AND I ENJOY A **PASSIONATE** NIGHT TOGETHER.

HEH HEH. ENJOY THE SHOW.

GET AWAY FROM HER, GEH-RU.

SHPAT

DIDN'T I TELL YOU TO STAY PUT? YOUR KIND MUST NOT HEAR VERY WELL.

YOU DAMN **PEASANT**!

SHPAT

I REALLY WANTED TO SHOW YOU OUR **SPECIAL** RELATIONSHIP.

I'LL KILL YOU!

Please wake up, Your Highness. I mean, Inspector.
We arrived at our destination **hours** ago.

Did you sleep well, Inspector?

I had a dream.
A dream about **me**? If you did, then it's a **good** dream.

Yes, it was. However, you didn't recognize me nor did you acknowledge my calling, saying I must continue my journey **alone**...
Really? Don't mind it, then. It's meaningless.
I'll **always** stay by your side. That's the **only** reason why I exist.
You always **WERE** by my side.
Always...

FOR MY PROTECTION...!

The resurrection of Ellea! Why, and for whom? Gadirok 2, COMING SOON...

REQUIEM CHORUS

First published in Korea in 2001 by DAIWON C.I. Inc.
English translation rights in USA, Canada, UK, IRIE, NZ, and Australia arranged by DAIWON C.I. Inc.

Translator JI SUN LEE
Lead Translator/Translation Dept. Supervisor JAVIER LOPEZ
ADV Manga Translation Staff JASON AN, TRISHA EGGLESTON AND SIMON JUNG

Print Production/ Art Studio Manager LISA PUCKETT
Pre-press Manager KLYS REEDYK
Art Production Manager RYAN MASON
Sr. Designer/Creative Manager JORGE ALVARADO
Graphic Designer/Group Leader SHANNON RASBERRY
Graphic Designer NANAKO TSUKIHASHI
Graphic Artists CHRIS LAPP, CHY LING, KRISTINA MILESKI AND NATALIA MORALES
Graphic Intern MARK MEZA

Publishing Editor SUSAN ITIN
Assistant Editor MARGARET SCHAROLD
Editorial Assistant VARSHA BHUCHAR
Proofreaders SHERIDAN JACOBS AND STEVEN REED
Research/ Traffic Coordinator MARSHA ARNOLD

Executive VP, CFO, COO KEVIN CORCORAN

President, CEO & Publisher JOHN LEDFORD

Email: editor@adv-manga.com
www.adv-manga.com
www.advfilms.com

For sales and distribution inquiries, please call 1.800.282.7202

ADV Manga™ is a division of A.D. Vision, Inc.
10114 W. Sam Houston Parkway, Suite 200, Houston, Texas 77099

ISBN: 1-4139-0068-2
First printing, July 2004
10 9 8 7 6 5 4 3 2 1
Printed in Canada

Gadirok Volume 1

Gadirok is a word from an old Korean dialect, which means "as time goes by" or "as we go along".

PG. 74 **So I've decided to go collect some offerings.**

Korea, as well as many other East Asian countries, was and still is heavily influenced by Buddhism. In the past, a Buddhist monk would depart from his temple to enter a village nearby to collect offerings. There were many kinds of offerings which were given to the monk: food, incense, among many other things. After the offerings were received, the monk would then bless their houses. It was a way for the local villagers to receive blessings and also pay their respects to the Buddha and the temple.

PG. 179 **A dream about me? If you did, then it's a good dream.**

Though the exact period when the Koreans' custom of interpreting their dreams began is unknown, Koreans have been interpreting their dreams for many centuries. Obviously, the interpretation of the dream and its relation to the person all depends on the dream itself. For example, if you come across a pig in your dream, then the dream is interpreted as a dream of good fortune. However, if you witness a wolf breaking into a pigsty in your dream, then it is interpreted as a dream of bad fortune, more specifically, a warning of a burglar breaking into your house.

Bibliography

Kim, San-Ho. *Dae-Jew-Shin-Jeh-Gook-Sah.* Seoul: Doosan Corporation, 2000.

Gunslinger Girl vol. 1	ISBN 1-4139-0020-8	$ 9.99
Happy Lesson vol. 1	ISBN 1-4139-0021-6	$ 9.99
Jinki: Extend vol. 1	ISBN 1-4139-0052-6	$ 9.99
Kagerou-Nostalgia: The Resurrection vol. 1	ISBN 1-4139-0053-4	$ 9.99
Louie The Rune Soldier vol. 1	ISBN 1-4139-0085-2	$ 9.99
Louie The Rune Soldier vol. 2	ISBN 1-4139- 0105-0	$ 9.99
Pretear vol. 1	ISBN 1-4139-0144-1	$ 9.99
RahXephon Bible Illustration Book	ISBN 1-4139-0026-7	$19.98
R^2 vol. 1	ISBN 1-4139-0056-9	$ 9.99
The Ruler of the Land vol. 1	ISBN 1-4139-0031-3	$ 9.99
The Ruler of the Land vol. 2	ISBN 1-4139-0037-2	$ 9.99
The Ruler of the Land vol. 3	ISBN 1-4139- 0057-7	$ 9.99
The Ruler of the Land vol. 4	ISBN 1-4139-0058-5	$ 9.99
Saint Marie vol. 1	ISBN 1-4139-0065-8	$ 9.99
Seven of Seven vol. 1	ISBN 1-4139-0008-9	$ 9.99
Seven of Seven vol. 2	ISBN 1-4139-0009-7	$ 9.99
Seven of Seven vol. 3	ISBN 1-4139-0010-0	$ 9.99
Sky Blade: Sword of the Heavens vol. 1	ISBN 1-4139-0081-X	$ 9.99
Sky Blade: Sword of the Heavens vol. 2	ISBN 1-4139-0102-6	$ 9.99
Steel Angel Kurumi vol. 1	ISBN 1-4139-0011-9	$ 9.99
Steel Angel Kurumi vol. 2	ISBN 1-4139-0012-7	$ 9.99
Steel Angel Kurumi vol. 3	ISBN 1-4139-0013-5	$ 9.99
Steel Angel Kurumi vol. 4	ISBN 1-4139-0059-3	$ 9.99
Steel Angel Kurumi vol. 5	ISBN 1-4139- 0078-X	$ 9.99
Steel Angel Kurumi vol. 6	ISBN 1-4139-0099-2	$ 9.99
Sweet & Sensitive vol. 1	ISBN 1-4139-0074-7	$ 9.99
Those Who Hunt Elves vol. 1	ISBN 1-4139-0014-3	$ 9.99
Those Who Hunt Elves vol. 2	ISBN 1-4139-0015-1	$ 9.99
Those Who Hunt Elves vol. 3	ISBN 1-4139-0034-8	$ 9.99
Those Who Hunt Elves vol. 4	ISBN 1-4139-0063-1	$ 9.99
Those Who Hunt Elves vol. 5	ISBN 1-4139-0077-1	$ 9.99
To Heart vol. 1	ISBN 1-4139-0022-4	$ 9.99
To Heart vol. 2	ISBN 1-4139-0070-4	$ 9.99
Your and My Secret vol. 1	ISBN 1-4139-0143-3	$ 9.99

One's just not enough.

MANGA SURVEY

PLEASE MAIL THE COMPLETED FORM TO: EDITOR – ADV MANGA
c/o A.D. Vision, Inc. 10114 W. Sam Houston Pkwy., Suite 200 Houston, TX 77099

Name:____
Address:______________________________________
City, State, Zip:_________________________________
____
E-Mail:____
Male ☐ Female ☐ Age:____________________

☐ ***CHECK HERE IF YOU WOULD LIKE TO RECEIVE OTHER INFORMATION OR FUTURE OFFERS FROM ADV.***

All information provided will be used for internal purposes only. We promise not to sell or otherwise divulge your information.

1. Annual Household Income (*Check only one*)

☐ Under $25,000
☐ $25,000 to $50,000
☐ $50,000 to $75,000
☐ Over $75,000

2. How do you hear about new Manga releases? (*Check all that apply*)

☐ Browsing in Store
☐ Internet Reviews
☐ Anime News Websites
☐ Direct Email Campaigns
☐ Online forums (message boards and chat rooms)
☐ Carrier pigeon
☐ Other:____________________________
☐ Magazine Ad
☐ Online Advertising
☐ Conventions
☐ TV Advertising

3. Which magazines do you read? (*Check all that apply*)

☐ Wizard
☐ SPIN
☐ Animerica
☐ Rolling Stone
☐ Maxim
☐ DC Comics
☐ URB
☐ Polygon
☐ Original Play Station Magazine
☐ Entertainment Weekly
☐ YRB
☐ EGM
☐ Newtype USA
☐ SciFi
☐ Starlog
☐ Wired
☐ Vice
☐ BPM
☐ I hate reading
☐ Other:________________

MGA/001

4. Have you visited the ADV Manga website?

☐ Yes
☐ No

5. Have you made any manga purchases online from the ADV website?

☐ Yes
☐ No

6. If you have visited the ADV Manga website, how would you rate your online experience?

☐ Excellent
☐ Good
☐ Average
☐ Poor

7. What genre of manga do you prefer?
(*Check all that apply*)

☐ adventure
☐ romance
☐ detective
☐ action
☐ horror
☐ sci-fi/fantasy
☐ sports
☐ comedy

8. How many manga titles have you purchased in the last 6 months?

☐ none
☐ 1-4
☐ 5-10
☐ 11+

9. Where do you make your manga purchases? (*Check all that apply*)

☐ comic store
☐ bookstore
☐ newsstand
☐ online
☐ other:_______________
☐ department store
☐ grocery store
☐ video store
☐ video game store

10. Which bookstores do you usually make your manga purchases at?
(*Check all that apply*)

☐ Barnes & Noble
☐ Walden Books
☐ Suncoast
☐ Best Buy
☐ Amazon.com
☐ Borders
☐ Books-A-Million
☐ Toys "Я" Us
☐ Other bookstore:
____

11. What's your favorite anime/manga website? (*Check all that apply*)

☐ adv-manga.com
☐ advfilms.com
☐ rightstuf.com
☐ animenewsservice.com
☐ animenewsnetwork.com
☐ Other:_______________
☐ animeondvd.com
☐ anipike.com
☐ animeonline.net
☐ planetanime.com
☐ animenation.com

All information provided will be used for internal purposes only. We promise not to sell or otherwise divulge your information.